D0342836

THE DREAMERS AND DACA

BY DUCHESS HARRIS, JD, PHD WITH NINA JUDITH KATZ

Essential Library

An Imprint of Abdo Publishing | abdobooks.com

abdobooks.com

Published by Abdo Publishing, a division of ABDO, PO Box 398166, Minneapolis, Minnesota 55439. Copyright © 2019 by Abdo Consulting Group, Inc. International copyrights reserved in all countries. No part of this book may be reproduced in any form without written permission from the publisher. Essential Library™ is a trademark and logo of Abdo Publishing.

Printed in the United States of America, North Mankato, Minnesota
092018
012019

THIS BOOK CONTAINS
RECYCLED MATERIALS

Cover Photo: Lynne Sladky/AP Images
Interior Photos: Chelsea Purgahn/Tyler Morning Telegraph/AP Images, 4–5; iStockphoto, 9, 26–27, 31, 71, 77; Andrey Popov/Shutterstock Images, 11; Ron Sachs/ Pool/Abacapress.com/Newscom, 14–15; Shutterstock Images, 16; Joel Martinez/ The Monitor/AP Images, 18; Ron Edmonds/AP Images, 20; Red Line Editorial, 23, 91; Marcio Jose Sanchez/AP Images, 25; Rodrigo Abd/AP Images, 28; North Wind Picture Archive, 34–35; Everett Historical/Shutterstock Images, 40; PhotoQuest/Archive Photos/Getty Images, 43; AP Images, 45; Mark Reinstein/Shutterstock Images, 49; Ken Tannenbaum/Shutterstock Images, 51; Evan Vucci/AP Images, 53; Rena Schild/ Shutterstock Images, 54–55; Kyodo/AP Images, 57; Thomas M Spindle/Shutterstock Images, 60; Jeff Chiu/AP Images, 62; Stephen Smith/Guest of a Guest/S/Newscom, 64; Alex Edelman/picture-alliance/dpa/AP Images, 67; Diego G Diaz/Shutterstock Images, 68–69; Matt Rourke/AP Images, 73; Eric Gay/AP Images, 75; Michael Brochstein/Sipa USA/AP Images, 78–79; Pablo Martinez Monsivais/AP Images, 83; Jose Luis Magana/AP Images, 87; John Roca/Polaris/Newscom, 88; Michael Nigro/ Sipa USA/Newscom, 92–93; Alex Wong/Getty Images News/Getty Images, 96; Pete Marovich/Getty Images News/Getty Images, 99

Editor: Alyssa Krekelberg
Series Designer: Maggie Villaume

Library of Congress Control Number: 2018948242

Publisher's Cataloging-in-Publication Data

Names: Harris, Duchess, author. | Katz, Nina Judith, author.
Title: The dreamers and DACA / by Duchess Harris and Nina Judith Katz.
Description: Minneapolis, Minnesota : Abdo Publishing, 2019 | Series: Special
        reports set 4 | Includes online resources and index.
Identifiers: ISBN 9781532116773 (lib. bdg.) | ISBN 9781532159619 (ebook)
Subjects: LCSH: Deportation--United States--Juvenile literature. | Undocumented
        aliens--Juvenile literature. | Adult children of immigrants--Juvenile literature. |
        Emigration and immigration law--Juvenile literature.
Classification: DDC 323.329--dc23

CONTENTS

CHAPTER ONE

A STORY OF
A DREAMER

Pratishtha Khanna was born in New Delhi, India—a place she described as "the land of temples and colorful festivals."[1] In 2002, when she was in middle school, her family moved to Maryland. Pratishtha's father, Raman, had moved there a year before to find better job opportunities. Pratishtha and her family all entered the country legally on tourist visas. With tourist visas, people are allowed to stay in the United States for only a limited time—most often up to six months. After Raman had arrived in the United States, his employer had begun the process of applying for a work visa for him. Work visas allow immigrants to find legal employment in the United States.

Thousands of undocumented immigrant children live in the United States.

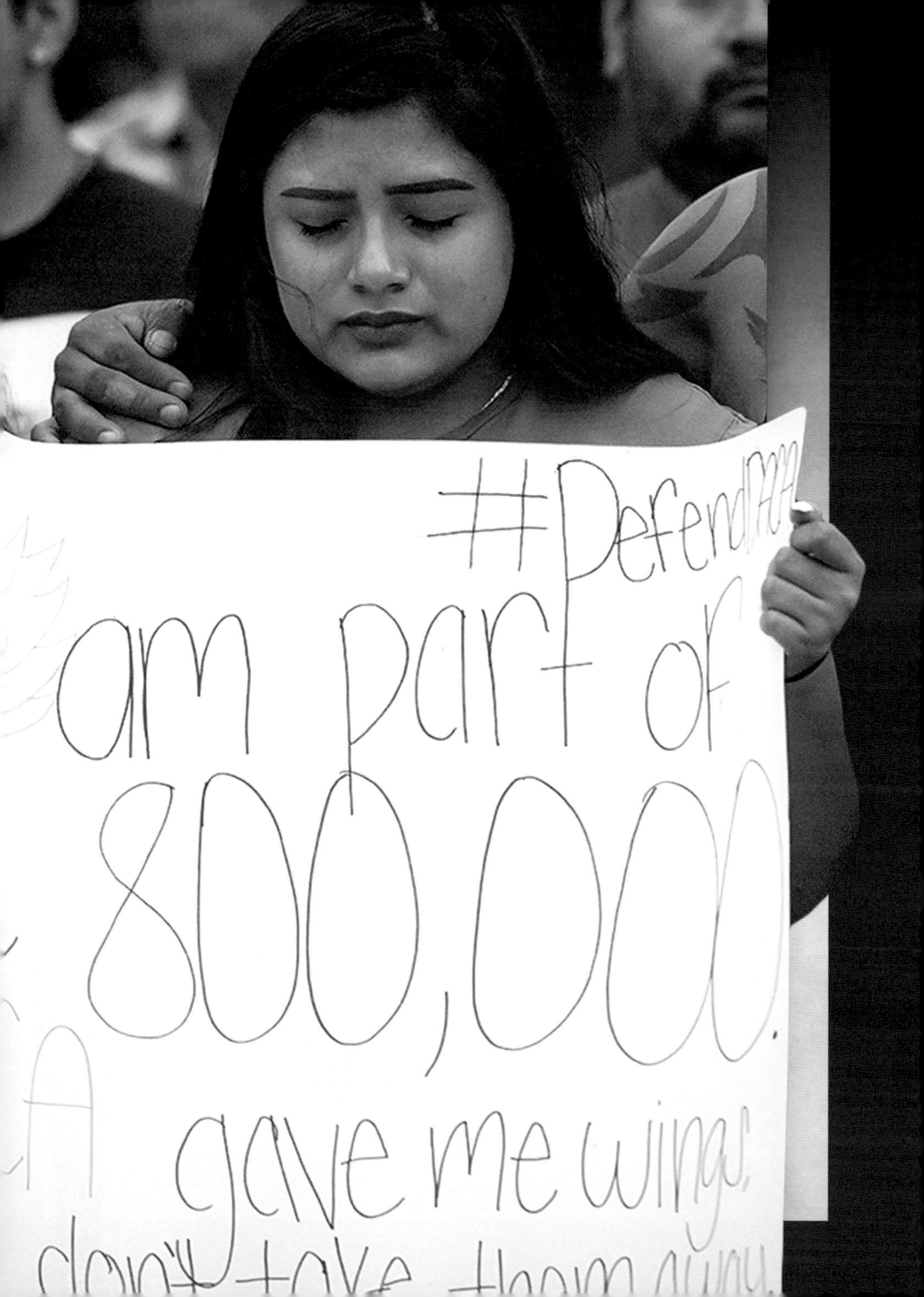
#Defend
am part of
800,000.
gave me wings;

MORE TO THE
STORY

APPLYING FOR VISAS

Applying for a visa is a complicated process. It begins by contacting the local US embassy or consulate, or visiting its website. Different US embassies and consulates have different rules about the visa application process. In general, the process begins with filling out and submitting an application together with a photograph and fee. Applicants also need to present valid passports from their countries of origin. The next step is scheduling an interview, although the interview is not required for children younger than 14 years or for adults older than 80 years. The wait for an interview varies significantly, depending on the country and city where the embassy or consulate is located. In some places, it is only one day, whereas in others it is almost one year. Usually, fingerprinting is also necessary. This may happen at the interview, or the applicants may have to do it separately. After the interview, the applicant may need to submit additional documentation or may hear that the application requires additional administrative processing. This can take another two months. If the visa is approved, there may be an additional visa insurance fee.

However, the visa itself does not guarantee entry into the United States. According to the US Department of State, having a visa allows a person to travel to a port of entry, such as a land-border crossing or an airport. The immigration officials at the port of entry will determine if that person can enter the country.

VISA STRUGGLE AND WORKER EXPLOITATION

Pratishtha recalls happy memories after arriving in the United States: "My early memories of America consist of joyful bus rides to middle school, constantly widening my eyes in blissful surprises as I assimilated to a completely different culture at school, meticulously organizing my school binder, and playing in eight feet [2.4 m] of snow during the blizzard of 2003—my first encounter with snow."[2] But the Khanna family was struggling. They were still waiting for visas so they could stay in the United States.

Without a work visa, an employer can exploit their workers. Often, it's difficult for an immigrant without legal standing to complain about low wages, lack of vacation days, or other work conditions that violate US labor law. Immigrants without legal standing depend on their

DIFFERENT KINDS OF VISAS

US visas are named in a combination of letters and numbers. Tourists come to the United States on tourist visas, which do not allow them to work and allow them to stay for only a short period. Students can come to the United States if they have student visas. These visas let them stay for a period to study, but they do not allow an immigrant student to work. A wide variety of specific work visas allow various workers to live and work in the United States for a period of time.

> "WE ARE AND ALWAYS WILL BE A NATION OF IMMIGRANTS. WE WERE STRANGERS ONCE, TOO. AND WHETHER OUR FOREBEARS WERE STRANGERS WHO CROSSED THE ATLANTIC, OR THE PACIFIC, OR THE RIO GRANDE, WE ARE HERE ONLY BECAUSE THIS COUNTRY WELCOMED THEM IN AND TAUGHT THEM THAT TO BE AN AMERICAN IS ABOUT SOMETHING MORE THAN WHAT WE LOOK LIKE, OR WHAT OUR LAST NAMES ARE, OR HOW WE WORSHIP."[3]
>
> **—PRESIDENT BARACK OBAMA, 2014**

employers. If they complain and the employer fires them, they might not find another job. If they try to organize with other workers for better benefits, the employer may contact immigration authorities and have them deported.

Time passed, and although the Khanna family didn't have visas, they were committed to living in the United States. Raman had lived in the United States for six years and his children had been attending school in the United States for five years. Raman wanted them to complete their education. Pratishtha was in the middle of high school and her brother was in elementary school. Her parents wanted them both to graduate and go on to college.

SEEKING AN EDUCATION

When it came time to apply to college, Pratishtha faced difficulties. Applications asked for her Social Security

8

Higher education provides more job opportunities for both immigrants and people who were born in the United States.

number, which she didn't have, so she had to leave that question blank. As a result, her applications couldn't be processed electronically. She had to fill them out by hand and add a note explaining that she was undocumented. Her grades were good and she hoped to attend the University of Maryland, Baltimore County. But Pratishtha wondered how she would pay for college.

Because Pratishtha was undocumented, she could not receive the scholarship she needed to go to college. Scholarship money often comes from the federal government. Students need either citizenship or a green card to be eligible. Without a Social Security number, Pratishtha couldn't even fill out the Free Application for Federal Student Aid (FAFSA) form required to apply for scholarships. She also couldn't get a decent-paying job to pay her way through college. This meant that four-year schools were out of reach. Pratishtha asked her teachers and high school guidance counselor what to do, but the only resources they knew of were for citizens and permanent residents. However, her mother, Seema, was determined to find a way for her daughter to go to college. "Two months before high school graduation my mother dragged me to a local community college in Maryland and forced me to knock on any door that might provide me with a gateway to college," said Pratishtha.[4]

Finally, Pratishtha found a program at Howard Community College in Maryland that required excellent grades and exam scores but did not require a Social Security number. Two weeks after applying, she received her acceptance letter. "That day was monumental," Pratishtha said, "I was no longer

GREEN CARDS

A green card grants an immigrant permanent residence, or the right to live in the United States continually. It does not grant citizenship. However, after five years, most green card holders become eligible to apply for citizenship. If someone is the spouse, fiancé(e), immediate family member, or widow or widower of a US citizen, he or she is eligible to apply for a green card. Immigrant workers are often eligible to apply for green cards as well. Refugees in the United States may also be eligible to apply for green cards.

Many college students rely on some form of financial aid to help pay for their schooling.

a 'shadow,' I was . . . a first generation, Indian (Asian) American college student."[5]

Pratishtha graduated high school in 2009 and started attending Howard Community College. Because she was undocumented, she wasn't eligible for in-state tuition and had to pay the higher costs of international tuition. To earn money, Pratishtha cleaned houses and tutored high school students. Between work and school, Pratishtha often put in 12- to 16-hour days. She completed her associate's degree in December 2011.

"OUR NATION'S IMMIGRATION LAWS MUST BE ENFORCED IN A FIRM AND SENSIBLE MANNER. BUT THEY ARE NOT DESIGNED TO BE BLINDLY ENFORCED. . . . NOR ARE THEY DESIGNED TO REMOVE PRODUCTIVE YOUNG PEOPLE TO COUNTRIES WHERE THEY MAY NOT HAVE LIVED OR EVEN SPEAK THE LANGUAGE."[6]

—JANET NAPOLITANO, SECRETARY OF HOMELAND SECURITY, 2012

Pratishtha hoped to transfer to the University of Maryland, but she was still ineligible for financial aid.

DACA BEGINS

On June 15, 2012, President Barack Obama announced a new policy for certain undocumented immigrants who had come to the United States as children. This policy came to be known as Deferred Action for Childhood Arrivals (DACA). If eligible, immigrants applied for DACA status and if the Department of Homeland Security approved their applications, they would then be free from the threat of deportation for two years. They could also apply for work visas. If they received a work visa, they could apply for a Social Security card. That, in turn, made them eligible to fill out FAFSA. Pratishtha applied for DACA status and was accepted. DACA

WHO COULD APPLY FOR DACA?

To be eligible to apply for DACA, an immigrant had to meet several criteria. First, immigrants had to have come to the United States before they were 16 years old. Second, they had to have lived in the United States since June 15, 2007. Immigrants also had to be younger than 31 years old and had to be at least 15 years old before applying. Applicants also needed to either be enrolled in school, be a high school graduate, or a veteran who was honorably discharged. In addition, immigrants could not have felonies or misdemeanors on their records, or have been a threat to people's safety or national security.

made it possible for Pratishtha to go to the University of Maryland, as she had longed to do for so many years. As of 2018, more than 800,000 people had received DACA status since the program began.[7]

The United States has a long history when it comes to debating immigration. Part of that history includes the government limiting immigrants' entry into the country based on their race. That's because the US government viewed some races as undesirable. People in the United States have varying opinions when it comes to immigration and what to do about undocumented immigrants.

OVERSTAYING A VISA AND DACA

Ivy Lei came to the United States from China at age seven. She clung to memories of orange-colored pork buns, egg custard with crème brûlée, and casinos—they were all she remembered of her hometown. Like Pratishtha, Ivy came to the United States legally and outstayed her visa.

When she first arrived, she accompanied her mother to her factory job. During factory inspections, Ivy would hide in a cabinet with rats, sometimes for hours. That's because there weren't supposed to be children in the factory. Later, Ivy was offered a full scholarship to the city university that she wanted to attend, but she could not accept because she had no Social Security number. Instead, she went to a less expensive university and worked part-time while earning a bachelor's degree in communications. Ivy writes, "When DACA was announced, my father cried . . . because his children finally had a shot at making something of their hard work, and my mother laughed because her resilience and optimism finally paid off."[8]

CHAPTER TWO

WHO ARE THE
DREAMERS?

President Obama introduced the DACA program in 2012 to protect the people known as Dreamers from deportation. Dreamers are long-term US residents who were brought to the United States as children. Many Dreamers came here legally but, like Pratishtha, they were unable to update their visas for various reasons. Other Dreamers were brought to the United States without visas. Most of the Dreamers grew up and attended school in the United States. Some Dreamers joined the US military and work in various professions.

The term *Dreamer* comes from a bipartisan proposal called the Development, Relief and Education for Alien Minors (DREAM) Act. Republican senator Orrin Hatch

President Obama met DACA recipients while he was president.

of Utah first introduced the DREAM Act on August 1, 2001. The bill enjoyed support from both Democrats and Republicans. It offered permanent residence status to a large number of undocumented immigrant teens, college students, and recent college graduates.

The bill would have given permanent residence status to people in various situations. First, it would have

Orrin Hatch has expressed his support for solutions to help Dreamers stay in the United States.

given residence to people who had turned 12 years old before the bill passed or completed an application before turning 21 years old. It also would have given residence to people who successfully completed high school or the equivalent, people who had been in the United States for the five years before the bill passed, and people who demonstrated "good moral character."[1] In addition, it would have applied to people who came to the United States as children, had been in the country for at least five years, graduated from high school, and had not committed certain crimes. The bill also offered permanent residence status to people who would have met these requirements during the four years before the bill passed and were either currently attending college or were recent college graduates.

The 2001 DREAM Act would also have repealed an earlier law that made undocumented immigrant students ineligible for reduced tuition at most state universities. In addition, it would have removed the threat of deportation from high school students who were likely to become eligible to apply for permanent residence under the

Dreamers can face struggles affording college without government aid.

DREAM Act. It also would have allowed them to work legally in the country.

The DREAM Act would have given permanent residence status to a large number of people. However, this bill was never brought to the full Senate for a floor vote. Even though it enjoyed support from people in both political parties, it remained controversial.

NEW DREAM ACT PROPOSALS

In July 2003, Hatch introduced a new version of the DREAM Act. This version was quite similar to the previous

DREAM Act. Some key differences in this version specified that an eligible immigrant had to have come to the United States before turning 16 years old and, from that age onward, could not have been ordered to leave the country by US authorities.

On February 9, 2004, the Senate Judiciary Committee—which in part reviews immigration-related bills proposed to the Senate—voted favorably on the bill. It recommended that the Senate pass it. However, when the Committee approved the DREAM Act, the Republican Party was sharply divided between people who wanted to restrict immigration and people who wanted to offer a path to legalization for certain immigrants. The party disagreed so much that it prevented the new version of the DREAM Act from coming to the Senate floor for a vote.

New versions of the DREAM Act were proposed through the years. In 2006 and again in 2007, President George W. Bush advocated for a broader immigration bill that incorporated many of the same provisions as previous DREAM Acts. The 2006 version of this bill was known as the Comprehensive Immigration Reform Act. It passed with bipartisan support in the Senate but failed in the

House of Representatives. In 2007, the next effort to pass an immigration bill to allow a path to legalization was introduced as an amendment to the Department of Defense Authorization Bill. This kind of bill authorizes funding for the US military and is usually uncontroversial. However, the bill didn't pass.

In 2008, Obama campaigned for president on a promise to prioritize immigration reform. In 2010, during Obama's presidency, yet another version of the DREAM Act was added as an amendment to the National Defense Authorization Bill—another bill to authorize funding for the US military. However, the National Defense Authorization Bill didn't pass because the DREAM Act was included.

INCLUDING THE DREAM ACT IN MILITARY BILLS

Why was the DREAM Act included in military spending bills in 2007 and 2010? The US legislative process allows amendments to bills, and the amendments do not have to relate to the bill in which they are included. Often, senators tack on amendments that will fund projects for their own states. Legislators can also use this process to slip in a relatively controversial bill, such as the DREAM Act, as part of a bill that Congress is likely to pass. Because the military cannot function without funding, military spending bills almost always pass. This seemed to offer the DREAM Act a higher likelihood of passing than it had otherwise, but was ultimately unsuccessful in those two cases.

President George W. Bush has said that immigrants make great contributions to the United States.

"THESE ARE YOUNG PEOPLE WHO STUDY IN OUR SCHOOLS, THEY PLAY IN OUR NEIGHBORHOODS, THEY'RE FRIENDS WITH OUR KIDS, THEY PLEDGE ALLEGIANCE TO OUR FLAG. THEY ARE AMERICANS IN THEIR HEART, IN THEIR MINDS, IN EVERY SINGLE WAY BUT ONE: ON PAPER. . . . IT MAKES NO SENSE TO EXPEL TALENTED YOUNG PEOPLE, WHO, FOR ALL INTENTS AND PURPOSES, ARE AMERICANS."[3]

—PRESIDENT BARACK OBAMA, JUNE 15, 2012

In December 2010, the DREAM Act passed the House of Representatives by a slim majority of 216–198.[2] However, the act never made it far enough in the Senate for a vote. In April 2012, Republican senator Marco Rubio began talking about a trimmed-down version of the DREAM Act. This version would offer a temporary visa rather than permanent residence to Dreamers. Some people believe Rubio's plans may have inspired Obama not to wait any longer. At this point, there had been years of effort to create a bill that could pass in Congress, and none had succeeded. On June 15, 2012, Obama announced the DACA policy that would bring relief to Dreamers across the country.

The first DACA recipients came from various regions, with most coming from Mexico and Central America.

WHERE THE FIRST DACA RECIPIENTS CAME FROM (2012-2013)[4]

COUNTRY OF BIRTH	NUMBER OF APPLICANTS	APPROVED FOR DACA
Mexico	348,579	57%
El Salvador	18,785	55%
Honduras	12,463	45%
Guatemala	11,672	52%
South Korea	7,007	76%
Peru	6,569	65%
Brazil	5,550	58%
Colombia	4,951	59%
Ecuador	4,787	60%
Philippines	3,296	70%
Argentina	2,941	61%
India	2,687	63%
Jamaica	2,556	40%
Venezuela	2,188	55%
Dominican Republic	2,014	46%
Trinidad and Tobago	1,923	46%
Bolivia	1,481	59%
Costa Rica	1,425	62%
Uruguay	1,294	65%
Pakistan	1,290	54%
Chile	1,223	61%
Poland	1,220	68%
Nicaragua	1,017	51%
Nigeria	1,017	56%
Guyana	1,008	53%

Percentage of DACA applicants from:	Mexico: 74.9%	Central America: 10%	South America: 6.9%	Asia: 4.2%
	Caribbean: 1.7%	Africa: 1%	Europe: 0.9%	

*Numbers do not equal 100% because of rounding.

FROM THE
HEADLINES

DREAMERS AND A SCIENCE FAIR

Yuliana Huicochea moved to Phoenix, Arizona, from Mexico with her parents at age four. In high school she joined the science team. In 2002, her team took its solar boat to a national science competition in Buffalo, New York. Their teacher organized a trip to Niagara Falls, but immigration officers stopped Yuliana and three of her teammates near the Canadian border. All four had come to the United States as small children and were undocumented. The immigration officials grilled them with questions for hours.

Three of the students were younger than 18 years and were legally allowed to have a parent with them. However, the immigration authorities did not permit this. The officials even insulted them with racist slurs.

The immigration officials let the students go, but three years of deportation hearings followed. Yuliana was terrified of being sent back to Mexico. While at community college, she became an advocate for other undocumented immigrants. In July 2015, an immigration judge ruled that the students could stay in the country.

US Immigration and Customs Enforcement (ICE) is responsible for deporting people for violating immigration laws.

CHAPTER THREE

UNDOCUMENTED

People sometimes refer to undocumented immigrants as *illegal immigrants* or *illegal aliens*, but immigration reform supporters note that those terms are dehumanizing. Instead, they encourage people to say *undocumented immigrants*.

Holocaust survivor and award-winning author Elie Wiesel was vocal in his belief that proper terminology for immigrants was important. National Public Radio anchor María Hinojosa reported on a conversation with Wiesel on this subject:

> [Wiesel] said, "María, don't ever use the term 'illegal immigrant.'" And I said, "Why?" And he said, "Because once you label a people 'illegal,' that is exactly what the Nazis did to Jews. You do not label a people 'illegal.' They have committed an illegal act. They are immigrants who crossed illegally. They are immigrants who crossed without papers. They are immigrants who crossed without permission. They

Some immigrants are stopped by border-control agents if they illegally enter the United States.

Many immigrants from Central America are fleeing extreme violence in their home countries.

are living in this country without permission. But they are not an illegal people."[1]

Some undocumented immigrants come to the United States without visas. Others come on legal visas but outstay them. And some, such as Pratishtha and her family, come to the United States legally and try to follow legal procedures to extend their stay but are unsuccessful. As a result, the immigrants in these situations end up lacking legal status. As the Khanna story illustrates, that means undocumented immigrants cannot work legally and are not eligible for financial aid to continue their education.

WHERE ARE UNDOCUMENTED IMMIGRANTS COMING FROM?

The majority of immigrants who arrive in the United States without visas come from Mexico or Central America. People crossing the US–Mexico border illegally are often refugees fleeing gang violence or severe poverty in their home countries. For example, the city of San Pedro Sula in Honduras had a murder rate of 180 per 100,000 in 2014.[2] That murder rate is quite high compared with other countries'. The murder rates in three of the safest countries, Singapore, Switzerland, and Japan, are less than one per 100,000.[3] The murder rate in the United States was 4.9 per 100,000 in 2015.[4]

People also come to the United States legally but outstay their visas. According to the

REFUGEES VS. IMMIGRANTS

Immigrants include people who leave one country for another for a wide variety of reasons. Some people may come to join relatives, whereas others want to pursue professional goals. Refugees flee their native land because of danger. For example, gang violence in El Salvador, Honduras, and Guatemala pushes many people to flee as refugees. According to the United Nations High Commissioner for Refugees, refugees also include people fleeing their country because of a "well-founded fear of being persecuted because of his or her: Race; Religion; Nationality; Membership of a particular social group; or Political opinion."[5] International law says that refugees are entitled to protection and countries that refugees flee to cannot force them to return to their countries of origin.

> "I HAD NO OTHER CHOICE, I FELT I WAS RISKING MY LIFE AND MY CHILDREN'S LIVES TO CONTINUE STAYING THERE."[8]
>
> **—GUADALUPE, A WOMAN WHO FLED EL SALVADOR WITH HER TWO YOUNG CHILDREN IN NOVEMBER 2016**

US Department of Homeland Security, 1.17 percent of people who come to the United States legally on nonimmigrant visas overstay these visas.[6] Nonimmigrant visas include tourist visas, student visas, certain work visas, and other visas on which people come to the United States for a limited period with the intention of leaving again. According to the US Department of Homeland Security, Canada has the highest overall number of citizens outstaying their US visas, with a total of 119,418 overstays in 2016. This is more than twice the number for Mexican citizens in the United States, which had 46,658 overstays for the same year.[7]

THE EUROPEAN AND NON-EUROPEAN EXPERIENCE

Undocumented European and non-European immigrants can have different experiences in the United States. For example, a 2007 article in the *Los Angeles Times* reported on the positive stereotypes that made an Irish immigrant's

White undocumented immigrants typically face less discrimination than immigrants of color.

experience easier. Mary Brennan was an undocumented Irish immigrant who works as a nurse's aide. "When I tell people I'm undocumented, it shocks them," she said. "They think of JFK or Ronald Reagan, and they can't understand how an Irish person could be illegal."[9]

Still, Brennan's status has had a real effect on her life. She had to miss her brother's funeral in Ireland. She was

GIVING BACK TO SOCIETY

Jose Manuel Santoyo came to the United States from Mexico at age eight. DACA allowed him to study at Southern Methodist University in Texas, where he was the commencement speaker at his graduation. He writes, "I want to be able to work and I want to work in public service. . . . My education wasn't for me. My education was so that I could contribute to society. My education was so that I could give back to the community that has given me so much, to the country that has given me so much."[10]

afraid that if she left the United States and then applied for a visa to return, her application would be denied because of her previous undocumented status. As a white European, she experiences less prejudice than immigrants from Latin America, Asia, and Africa, but her undocumented status still complicates her life. It left her facing the threat of deportation, even after living and working in the United States for almost 17 years.

LACKING LEGAL STATUS

The number of immigrants without valid visas had reached its highest in 2007, when it was 12.2 million—or 4 percent of the US population. Under DACA, the number of immigrants lacking legal status declined notably. According to the Pew Research Center, in 2015 there were 300,000 fewer immigrants lacking legal status than in 2009. In 2009, Mexicans comprised 6.4 million of the immigrants without legal standing. By 2015, Mexicans comprised only 5.6 million.[11]

Immigrants without legal standing made up approximately 5 percent of people working or looking for work in the United States in 2014.[12] They worked predominantly in agriculture and construction. People who support deporting undocumented immigrants frequently claim that these immigrants take away jobs from US citizens. However, these immigrants generally work at jobs that US citizens do not want and in industries that need their labor.

CHAPTER FOUR

A HISTORY OF
IMMIGRATION

The United States has a history of restricting both citizenship and immigration to the country based on race. As of 1790, to become a citizen, immigrants had to be white, free, and "of good character."[1] They also had to live in the United States for a certain number of years before becoming citizens. Towns and states managed immigration without much involvement from the federal government. The borders stayed relatively open, although the 1790 requirement of whiteness for naturalization remained.

Many people came to North America voluntarily from Europe. Beginning in the 1500s, early colonists came to North America from Spain, France, England, and Holland. People of all classes came, ranging from

The United States has a long history of receiving immigrants who are seeking refuge.

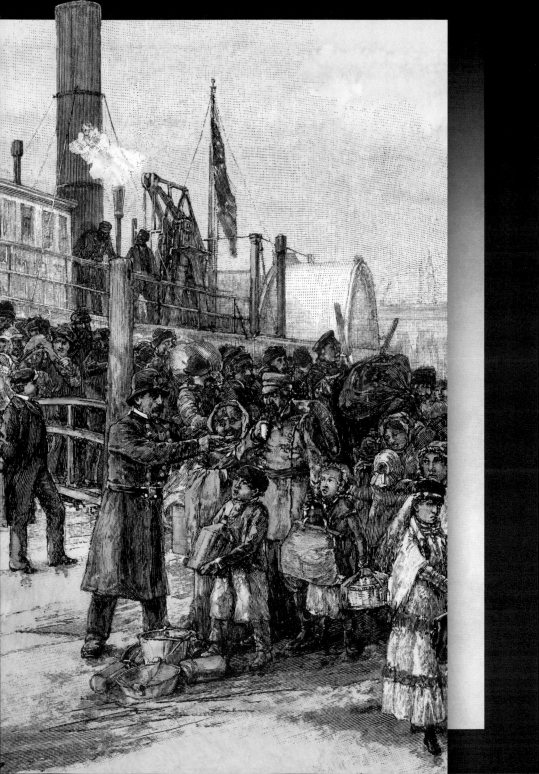

aristocrats to indentured servants. They were joined by people from Ireland, who varied in class status as well. Other early settlers came from Sweden, Poland, Germany, Italy, and Switzerland. Some people came to North America for religious freedom. Many came for economic reasons, just as many immigrants do today.

In addition to the Europeans who came voluntarily, approximately 388,000 people were kidnapped, enslaved, and brought to North America from Africa by force between the mid-1600s and 1860.[2] Some people managed to escape or buy their freedom. In 1790, there were only 60,000 African Americans living in the United States who were not enslaved.[3] The US government took measures to deny them citizenship.

EUROPEAN IMMIGRATION IN THE 1800s AND 1900s

In the 1800s, most immigrants came to the United States from Ireland and Germany. Approximately 4.5 million people came from Ireland between 1820 and 1930.[4] Most of them came for economic reasons—particularly in the years following a brutal potato famine that began in 1845. They faced discrimination, including signs outside of businesses saying, "No Irish need apply."[5] People opposing the new immigrants from Ireland founded the Know-Nothing Party. The Know-Nothings required their members to oppose Catholicism, which was the religion of many Irish immigrants, and to vote only for political candidates born in the United States. They wanted to change the law to require that people live in the United States for 25 years before they could apply for citizenship.

Six million people came to the United States from Germany between 1830 and 1930.[6] Although German immigrants did not face the same degree of prejudice as the Irish, they did face some. Anti-German bias came from both Anglo-Americans and Irish immigrants. Most German

THE POTATO FAMINE

The potato famine began in Ireland in September 1845. This famine occurred when a disease infected potato crops and destroyed them. Potatoes were a substantial part of the Irish population's diet. Through the next two years, many people became homeless. They ate bark, rats, and dogs. Smallpox, typhus, and other diseases spread, as did crime. Whole families died. Although some people stole food to eat, others committed crimes in the hopes of being imprisoned and fed. Hundreds of thousands left Ireland in ships overcrowded with ill passengers. These were called coffin ships because of their extraordinarily high death rate. England provided aid but in return took Irish farms and began exporting grain from Ireland while the local population was starving. At least one million people died.[7]

immigrants came to the United States for economic reasons, but some came as political refugees.

In addition, many people disliked immigrants from southern, central, and eastern Europe who came to the United States. Between 1820 and 1963, more than five million Italians came to the United States, with most of them arriving after 1880.[8] They came for economic reasons. The same period saw many Polish, Lithuanian, Latvian, Greek, Russian, Turkish, Armenian, Czech, Hungarian, Austrian, and Jewish immigrants arrive in the United States. These new arrivals also faced prejudice.

PREJUDICE TOWARD ASIAN IMMIGRANTS

Asian immigrants faced significant prejudice in the United States. Chinese, Filipino, Malay, and Japanese people came to the United States as merchants, sailors, and crew members starting in the late 1700s. Some became naturalized. At the same time, intolerance toward Asian immigrants was widespread in the United States. Sometimes the white people in a town massacred their Asian neighbors or forced them to move out.

The largest numbers of Chinese immigrants came during the California Gold Rush. In 1852 alone, more than 20,000 Chinese immigrants came to California. By 1870, the United States was home to 63,000 Chinese immigrants. Seventy-seven percent of them lived in California.[9]

Some Chinese immigrants came to the United States in the mid-1800s as indentured servants. Southern plantation owners welcomed them after the Civil War (1861–1865) because they wanted free indentured workers to replace the newly freed African American people. Chinese people were initially allowed to enter the country without restriction, but they could not usually become citizens.

NOT WHITE ENOUGH FOR CITIZENSHIP

Takao Ozawa came to the United States from Japan in 1894. He completed high school in Berkeley, California, and went to the University of California. In 1914, he applied for citizenship. When his application was turned down, he took it to court. The court was explicit that race was the only reason for denying his application but still upheld the denial on the grounds that US law required whiteness for naturalization. Ozawa appealed to the Supreme Court, where he argued that he should be recognized as American because of his US education, his use of English, his lack of connections to Japan, and also the whiteness of his skin. In 1917, the Supreme Court ruled that the 1790 Naturalization Act authorized the naturalization of white people and that Ozawa was not white. Therefore, he could not become naturalized.

US GOVERNMENT INVOLVEMENT

After the Civil War, the US federal government began to take charge of immigration and naturalization. Up until that point, the individual states had more control over naturalization. In 1882, the United States passed the Chinese Exclusion Act, the first of a series of laws limiting immigration from China. Chinese immigrants had to fill out endless forms to prove that they were able bodied. They also had to prove that they belonged to one of the small

President Chester A. Arthur signed the Chinese Exclusion Act.

number of categories of Chinese people allowed to come to the United States. They had to be merchants, teachers, students, travelers, diplomats, or immediate relatives of people born in the United States. Many people made false claims to get into the United States. A large industry developed to provide papers "proving" that Chinese immigrants had parents born in the United States. All Asian immigrants faced some discrimination in the United States. A 1790 law still prevented them from becoming citizens, and they faced discrimination in housing, stores, churches, and many other places and situations.

The parallels between these immigrants and current undocumented immigrants are notable. In both cases, the immigration system favors the immediate relatives of US citizens as well as diplomats, members of certain prestigious professions, and short-term travelers.

In 1910, the Angel Island Immigration Station opened on an island in San Francisco Bay, California. Asian immigrants went there when they reached the West Coast. There, they were detained for periods of time—typically ranging from two weeks to six months.

Because of the Chinese Exclusion Act, Chinese immigrants received the worst treatment at Angel Island compared with other immigrants. The act was intended to exclude Chinese people from the United States, and the immigration authorities looked for reasons to do just that. Doctors and nurses stripped them and inspected them for signs of disease and physical defects. They measured various parts of their bodies to guess their age. Next, immigration officials interrogated them to try to find out whether they really were merchants, immediate family members of US nationals, or otherwise part of the small group of Chinese people legally allowed to come to the United States.

People claiming to be merchants needed two non-Chinese witnesses to testify about their business. They also needed documents showing what they were selling and who their business partners were. Chinese immigrants claiming family relationships sometimes had to draw maps of their hometowns. Immigration authorities asked them who lived in which house in which row in their hometown. They also had to state the birth and marriage dates for distant family members. If two people from the same family, for example, gave any answers that differed from each other in the slightest detail, the immigration authorities took the difference as proof that the people applying for immigration were not really the relatives or spouses of the people with whom they were claiming that relationship. The Chinese Exclusion Act remained law until 1943, when Congress repealed it because China had become an ally in World War II (1939–1945).

LIMITING IMMIGRATION

Before the Chinese Exclusion Act was repealed, Congress passed additional laws restricting immigration. In 1921, Congress passed the Emergency Quota Act, limiting immigration to 198,081 people per year from Northern and

Asian immigrants were interviewed at Angel Island Immigration Station to determine whether they could enter the United States.

Western Europe, which was predominantly Protestant. The act also limited immigration to 158,367 people per year from all the other countries in the Eastern Hemisphere. The next year, Congress drastically lowered the numbers. Only 140,999 people would be admitted from Northern and Western Europe and only 21,847 from the rest of the Eastern Hemisphere.[10] Congress set no limits on immigration from the Americas.

In 1924, Congress introduced more specific quotas. These quotas allowed up to 65,361 people from Great Britain and Northern Ireland, which was predominantly Protestant, up to 25,814 people from Germany, up to 25,814 from the Republic of Ireland, which is predominantly Catholic, and up to 40,483 from all the rest of Europe combined.[11] Congress intended the quotas to encourage Protestant immigration while minimizing Catholic, Jewish, Asian, and African immigration.

Most Asian and African countries each had quotas of only 100 people.[12] Although there was no limit on immigration from the Americas, nonwhite Asians coming to the United States through Canada or Mexico counted under the quota for their country of ancestral origin rather than as Canadians or Mexicans. If even one-half of a person's ancestors hailed from anywhere in Asia or the Pacific Islands, the person could be admitted only under the quota for the ancestral country of the Asian or Pacific ancestors.

In addition, in 1919 and 1927, US Representative John Box of Texas, a Democrat, proposed legislation to prohibit any Mexicans from becoming US citizens. During this period, the government organized mass deportations of Mexicans.

Later on, US quotas kept out most refugees from the Holocaust. However, in 1948, the United States accepted

A large number of Mexican immigrants worked on US farms in the early 1900s.

400,000 refugees who had lost their homes in World War II.[13]

In 1952, a new immigration act finally eliminated the racist rules preventing people from Asia from becoming citizens. However, the same law reaffirmed the quota system. President Harry Truman vetoed the bill because of this, but Congress supported it strongly enough to pass the bill over his veto.

Both as a senator and as president, John F. Kennedy argued for changing the quota system. He wrote, "The national origins quota system has strong overtones of an indefensible racial preference. It is strongly weighted toward so-called Anglo-Saxons."[14] Kennedy worked to have a new immigration law passed, but he was assassinated in 1963 before it could become law.

President Lyndon B. Johnson signed the new Immigration and Nationality Act of 1965, ending the ethnically

"THE IDEA BEHIND THIS DISCRIMINATORY POLICY WAS, TO PUT IT BOLDLY, THAT AMERICANS WITH ENGLISH OR IRISH NAMES WERE BETTER PEOPLE AND BETTER CITIZENS THAN AMERICANS WITH ITALIAN OR GREEK OR POLISH NAMES. . . . SUCH A CONCEPT IS UTTERLY UNWORTHY OF OUR TRADITIONS AND OUR IDEALS."[15]

—PRESIDENT HARRY TRUMAN ON THE IMMIGRATION AND NATIONALITY ACT OF 1952

based quota system. The Immigration and Nationality Act of 1965 allowed in a maximum of 170,000 people from the Eastern Hemisphere—including people from places such as Europe, Asia, Africa, Australia, and New Zealand—and 120,000 from the Western Hemisphere, such as people from Canada, Central America, and South America.[16]

MEXICO, CENTRAL AMERICA, AND SOUTH AMERICA

The Immigration and Nationality Act of 1965 was the first limit on the number of people allowed to enter the United States from the Americas. Open borders had previously allowed workers to enter the United States in search of employment.

In 1942, the United States and Mexico had launched the Bracero Program specifically to

"TODAY MANY OF OUR NEWCOMERS ARE FROM MEXICO AND PUERTO RICO. WE SOMETIMES FORGET THAT PUERTO RICANS ARE US CITIZENS BY BIRTH AND THEREFORE CANNOT BE CONSIDERED IMMIGRANTS. NONETHELESS, THEY OFTEN RECEIVE THE SAME DISCRIMINATORY TREATMENT . . . THAT WERE FACED BY OTHER WAVES OF NEWCOMERS. THE SAME THINGS ARE SAID TODAY OF PUERTO RICANS AND MEXICANS THAT WERE ONCE SAID OF IRISH, ITALIANS, GERMANS AND JEWS: 'THEY'LL NEVER ADJUST; THEY CAN'T LEARN THE LANGUAGE; THEY WON'T BE ABSORBED.'"[17]

—JOHN F. KENNEDY, 1964

bring Mexican men to the United States on work contracts. This was to help address labor shortages in the United States caused by World War II. The program continued after the war because many Mexicans needed paid work and were willing to accept difficult working conditions at low pay. Millions of Mexican men came to the United States under this program, which ended in 1964. The end of the Bracero Program, along with the new limit on immigration from the Americas in 1965, led to a sharp rise in undocumented immigration. Many employers welcomed undocumented immigrants, who now had no protective contracts and whom they could therefore exploit with lower wages.

Other factors led to a dramatic increase in immigration to the United States from Central and South America. These factors included economic troubles, poverty, political instability, and natural disasters.

BILLS ON IMMIGRATION

Democratic senator Ted Kennedy and Republican president Ronald Reagan worked together to create the Immigration Reform and Control Act, which Congress

Ronald Reagan supported tighter security at the US–Mexico border.

passed and Reagan signed in 1986. The act granted legal

status to undocumented immigrants already in the United

States while setting up a system to limit undocumented

immigration in the future. The system called for punishing

employers who hired undocumented workers. For the

next few years after this law was passed, there was

significantly less undocumented immigration. However,

the government never carried out the planned crackdown

on employers, and in the 1990s, undocumented

immigration began increasing again.

In 1996, Congress passed and President Bill Clinton signed a bill relating to immigration. It prevented undocumented immigrants—as well as some documented immigrants—from receiving food stamps and various other forms of public assistance. It also increased border control and deportation enforcement. In addition, it introduced rules requiring undocumented immigrants who left or were deported to stay outside of the United States for three or ten years, depending on how long they were in the country while undocumented, before applying for a visa to return.

In 2001, George W. Bush became president. He had campaigned on a promise of "compassionate conservatism."[18] He viewed undocumented immigration as a problem caused by inadequate laws and wanted solutions that would make it legal for people to cross the border to work in the United States. Then, the September 11, 2001, terrorist attacks occurred. A small group of people who had legally entered the United States hijacked four planes. They flew two of them into the World Trade Center in New York City and one into the Pentagon

The World Trade Center attack was the deadliest part of the September 11, 2001, terrorist attacks.

building in Washington, DC. Another plane crashed in a Pennsylvania field. Almost 3,000 people were killed.[19]

Six months later, the Immigration and Naturalization Service approved student visa applications for two of the 9/11 hijackers. The two were already dead—and infamous. Shocked and horrified by the bureaucratic error, Bush reorganized how the United States handled immigration. He had created the Department of Homeland

Security in response to 9/11, and he gave responsibility for immigration and naturalization requests to this new agency. Customs and Border Protection (CBP) and Immigration and Customs Enforcement (ICE) became new organizations within the Department of Homeland Security. The visa application process changed and became much more cumbersome for people from many countries. People from most non-Western countries now had to go through an interview at a US embassy to get a visa. Because the 9/11 hijackers were young Muslim men, new regulations required young men from predominantly Muslim countries, whether they themselves were Muslim or not, to fill out a detailed questionnaire and provide a large amount of personal information about their families, finances, and other matters. The consequences of overstaying a visa became much more severe, and deportations became far more common. Some people in the government believe that these new rules help prevent terrorists from entering the country.

In his second term, Bush pushed for a bill that would include all of the earlier DREAM Act provisions to allow certain young people who entered the country as children and lacked legal standing to acquire legal documentation. He advocated for the bill to create a new guest worker program as well. President Obama continued the same approach to immigration that Bush and Reagan had championed. He advocated for the DREAM Act for years and then introduced the DACA program in 2012. The act was to give Dreamers relief from the threat of deportation. It also gave them a way to pursue educational and work opportunities.

As president, Obama strived to help Dreamers succeed in the United States.

CHAPTER FIVE

VIEWS ON
IMMIGRATION

H istorically, US immigration rules have changed in response to world events. For example, during World War II, fear and racism led to the incarceration of Japanese Americans. And the September 11, 2001, terrorist attacks sparked new concerns and debates about borders and safety that continued into the 2010s.

Many Americans have strong feelings about immigration. They tend to see any immigration policy, including DACA, through the lens of those feelings. The debate about immigration involves many questions of policies, principles, and religious beliefs.

Immigration supporters rallied in Portland, Oregon, in 2018.

QUESTIONS ON IMMIGRATION AND REFUGEES

People ask a variety of questions regarding immigration.
They wonder whether US immigration policy should be
largely open, mostly closed, or somewhere in between.
Some people, including members of President Donald
Trump's administration, have started to question whether
immigration policies should continue to allow the
close family members of people already living in the
United States to come to the country. This is known as
chain migration, or family reunification. John Burnett
of National Public Radio says, "the president claims that
chain migration takes jobs from Americans and threatens
national security. . . . What [Trump and his supporters]
want—it's called a merit-based scheme. . . . It gives
preference to job training and English proficiency and
education."[1]

What the United States should do with refugees
is another topic that people debate. Politicians and
US citizens question whether the county should even
welcome refugees. And if the United States does welcome
refugees, people ask whether it should welcome all

Since 2011, millions of Syrian refugees have fled the conflict in their country.

refugees equally. They ask whether it's fair to favor refugees or immigrants from some countries over those from other places. If favoritism is fair, should it be based on the needs of the refugees or immigrants themselves, or should US policy favor immigrants and refugees whom Americans perceive as more likely to be an asset to their country?

How people answer these questions usually depends on their attitudes toward immigrants, refugees, and, more broadly, on their feelings toward people who they perceive are different from themselves. Some people want to make sure that the United States changes as little as possible. President Kennedy noted in the 1960s, "In 1797

"STUDY AFTER STUDY REINFORCES THE NOTION THAT IMMIGRATION MAKES NATIVE-BORN AMERICANS BETTER OFF ON A WIDE RANGE OF EFFECTS—INNOVATION, THE PRICE OF GOODS AND SERVICES, THE NUMBER OF JOBS, GOVERNMENT FINANCES, AND EVEN WAGES. ACROSS THE BOARD, THE OVERWHELMING BULK OF EVIDENCE POINTS TO IMPROVED LIVELIHOODS FOR AMERICANS."[3]

—BENJAMIN HARRIS, A WRITER IN *FORTUNE* MAGAZINE

a member of Congress argued that, while a liberal immigration policy was fine when the country was new and unsettled, now that America had reached its maturity and was fully populated, immigration should stop."[2]

As different waves of immigrants came to the United States over the decades, people feared that immigrants would never learn English or assimilate into US culture. In fact, there have always been older immigrants who did not learn English but managed to operate in the United States with the help of their family members and communities. However, younger generations have an easier time learning English and growing up in US society. In addition, when kids grow up bilingual, they benefit from the cultural richness of two or more backgrounds. Several studies conducted in the 2000s measuring verbal intelligence, executive control, and some nonverbal skills have shown advantages to bilingualism.

FAVORITISM AND RACISM

Some anti-immigrant feelings border on racism, as the Chinese Exclusion Act illustrated. Some people today agree with race-based quotas. In her 2015 book *Adios, America,* Ann Coulter writes that the Immigration and Nationality Act of 1965 "snuffed out the generous quotas for immigrants from the countries that had traditionally populated America—England, Ireland, and Germany— and added 'family reunification' policies, allowing recent immigrants to bring in their relatives, and those relatives to bring in *their* relatives, until entire Somali villages have relocated to Minneapolis and Muslim cabdrivers are refusing to transport passengers with dogs or alcohol."[4]

Coulter's preference for English, Irish, and German immigrants is clear, and so is her discomfort with Africans and Muslims. These racial and

DIFFERENT IMMIGRANT GROUPS, DIFFERENT REACTIONS

A 2015 Pew Research report showed that Americans hold different views on immigrants from different countries. The study showed that 47 percent of Americans "expressed mostly positive views" when it came to European and Asian immigrants. However, only approximately 25 percent of Americans had the same feelings when it came to Latin American and African immigrants.[5]

Some people support tighter border security to keep immigrants from coming into the United States.

religious prejudices color her wish for an immigration system along the lines of the one from 1924, with its national quotas favoring immigrants from England, Ireland, and Germany, restricting those from the rest of Europe, and minimizing those from Asia and Africa. That 1924 quota system was intended to favor Protestants while limiting Catholic and Jewish immigration.

Coulter is far from the only person who wishes to ban certain immigrants from entering the United States. In 2015, a press release from Trump's presidential campaign noted, "Donald J. Trump is calling for a total and complete shutdown of Muslims entering the United States."[6] After becoming president, Trump tried to stop people from some countries with Muslim majorities from entering the United States.

SUCCESS, CONTRIBUTIONS, AND BENEFITS

Ali Noorani is the executive director of the National Immigration Forum (NIF). NIF is an organization that supports immigration to the United States. Noorani describes a 2011 conference that NIF organized with 200 conservative leaders. These leaders included politicians, religious leaders, business executives, and people from law enforcement. He writes, "They shared stories about the immigrants they knew. They spoke of families who were making their congregations and communities a more vibrant place, men and women from other countries they saw not as employees or constituents but as extended family. They spoke of immigrants in their

IMMIGRANTS CONTRIBUTING TO THE ECONOMY

Javier Noris came to the United States from Mexico when he was five years old. When he was older, he found a job at a convenience store. When DACA passed, he went to California State University, Northridge, to study economics and biotechnology. Then he found a job as a software engineer. A few years later, he became the CEO of a venture capital fund that supports start-up companies in science and technology.

neighborhoods who faced the threat of deportation, who faced prejudice, who faced a steep climb to the American dream they sought for their children."[7]

However, not everyone believes that all immigrants can succeed in the United States. People sometimes point to statistics claiming that a high percentage of immigrants rely on welfare. The studies most often cited to demonstrate this come from the Center for Immigration Studies (CIS). Both the Southern Poverty Law Center (SPLC), a legal advocacy group focused on civil rights, and the

Sundar Pichai is the CEO of Google. He is also an Indian immigrant.

Anti-Defamation League (ADL), a Jewish organization that works to stop anti-Semitism and hate crimes, have denounced CIS as a hate group. Immigration analysts have argued that CIS manipulates data to support anti-immigrant claims.

The CATO Institute, a libertarian research organization, said in 2018 that, "Overall, immigrants are less likely to consume welfare benefits and, when they do, they generally consume a lower dollar value of benefits than native-born Americans." It added that in 2016, the average welfare cost for immigrants was around $3,718, which was 39 percent less than the average cost for native-born Americans on welfare.[8]

HATE GROUP: THE CIS

The SPLC and the ADL both track hate groups. According to the SPLC, a hate group is an organization that condemns people based on their religion, race, sexual orientation, ethnicity, or gender identity. Both the SPLC and the ADL identify the CIS as a hate group, although the CIS calls itself a research center. The SPLC notes that the CIS publishes the work of white nationalists and anti-Semites, and that it manipulates data to support its arguments against immigration. However, the CIS's influence is widespread.

Stephen Miller, an adviser to President Trump, cites the CIS in support of his anti-immigration views. Also, *American Renaissance*, a white supremacist journal that both the SPLC and the ADL call out for racism and pseudoscientific articles, cites studies from the CIS. The CIS is also one of the main sources cited by Coulter in her book opposing immigration. The SPLC has also called out Coulter for white nationalism, and the ADL has found white nationalism, anti-Latino attacks, anti-immigrant bias, and anti-Semitism in her books and statements.

Immigrants make various contributions to the United States. For example, immigrants help the economy in many ways. The American Civil Liberties Union, a nonprofit that focuses on protecting people's rights, says, "Contrary to popular belief, immigrants do not take away jobs from American workers. Instead, they create new jobs by forming new businesses, spending their incomes on American goods and services, paying taxes and raising the productivity of U.S. businesses."[9] The National Foundation for American Policy, which is an organization that researches public policy, noted in 2016 that immigrants had founded more than 50 percent of start-up companies in the United States. Each start-up company has created an average of approximately 760 jobs.[10]

Thai Lee is the CEO of SHI International, an information technology company. She moved to the United States from South Korea as a teenager.

FROM THE HEADLINES

STRUGGLING THROUGH THE BIAS

Marielle Panizales moved with her family from the Philippines to Kuwait. Then, when Marielle was four years old, they moved to the United States. Her parents both worked as nurses. Like many immigrants, Marielle's parents were anxious about DACA and at first did not want Marielle to apply. They were afraid that the application itself might lead to deportation. But Marielle has had a positive experience with DACA. She notes that DACA provided her with opportunities, including the ability to work, get a driver's license, attend college, and help her parents out financially.

Marielle wants to share her story so other immigrants don't feel like they're alone. Writing for the Obama White House website on DACA, she notes the distinct troubles that plague US immigrants and says to them, "I know that you've probably worked hard your whole life and that learning what it means to be undocumented and all of the consequences that come with it can feel like the wind has been knocked out of you." Marielle adds that the media plays a large role in spreading hateful comments

In a show of support for DACA, people gathered in Washington, DC, in 2018 and held photos of DACA recipients.

toward undocumented immigrants: "I know the ignorant and spiteful comments, the dirty names and bullying, and the hate that gets thrown around in the media terrifies you. That I know that they want to build walls and throw us all out. . . . They don't realize the success and potential you have to offer, so you have to show them. I know that it can feel like you don't belong. But this is your country too. . . . Flowers can't bloom in the shadows and neither can you. There is an entire community of people that accept you and want to support you, you just have to open yourself to them."[11]

CHAPTER SIX

ARGUMENTS FOR
AND AGAINST
DACA

The majority of people in the United States support DACA. A 2018 poll done by CBS News showed that 87 percent of people surveyed wanted Dreamers to stay in the United States.[1] Supporters of DACA cite humanitarian reasons for allowing Dreamers to stay. A 2017 survey conducted by Tom Wong, an associate professor of political science from the University of California, San Diego, found that the average age of Dreamers was six-and-a-half years old when they came to the United States. In response to this finding, journalist Ilya Somin said, "The likely effect of deporting one of them . . . is only modestly less harsh

Many people believe the DACA program benefits the United States.

"I THINK OUR GOAL IS TO MAKE SURE WE'RE A WELCOMING COUNTRY. . . . AND THAT FOLKS HERE WHO COME HERE HAVE AN OPPORTUNITY TO LIVE THE AMERICAN DREAM, WHICH HAS ANIMATED PEOPLE FROM AROUND THE WORLD FOR GENERATIONS. THIS COUNTRY HAS BEEN A BEACON OF HOPE FOR PEOPLE STRUGGLING FROM THE VERY BEGINNING."[4]

—TIM PHILLIPS, PRESIDENT OF AMERICANS FOR PROSPERITY, A POLITICAL ADVOCACY ORGANIZATION

than deporting an otherwise comparable native-born American."[2]

Many people also give economic reasons for supporting DACA. Immigrants overall help the economy. But Dreamers in particular bring benefits. A fellow at the CATO Institute, Ike Brannon, said in 2018, "We expect in the next 10 years if we allow the DACA recipients to remain in the United States, that would add an extra $350 billion to the economy compared to excluding them from being able to work legally. And we also estimate that that would result in an additional $90 billion of tax revenue, just for the federal government."[3]

Opponents of DACA argue that immigrants are especially likely to commit crimes, although these statements have been broadly discredited by statistics. A 2006 article on the Heritage Foundation website, a conservative think tank that influences Republican

Many Dreamers end up working in high-skill professions, such as in health care.

policy positions, leads with the headline, "The Senate Immigration Bill Rewards Lawbreaking: Why the DREAM Act Is a Nightmare."[5] The article argues that Dreamers are lawbreakers because they are in the United States without documentation. And, as lawbreakers, they should be punished rather than rewarded with an opportunity to legalize their status or to attend school while paying in-state tuition.

Some people who believe strongly that anyone breaking immigration laws should face consequences argue that fines are the most appropriate form of penalty. For example, President Bush advocated for a path to

> "AS A PROSECUTOR, I CAN TELL YOU, IT IS A SERIOUS MISTAKE TO CONFLATE CRIMINAL JUSTICE POLICY WITH IMMIGRATION POLICY AS IF THEY ARE THE SAME THING. THEY ARE NOT. I HAVE PERSONALLY PROSECUTED EVERYTHING FROM LOW-LEVEL OFFENSES TO HOMICIDES. I KNOW WHAT A CRIME LOOKS LIKE. I WILL TELL YOU: AN UNDOCUMENTED IMMIGRANT IS NOT A CRIMINAL."[6]

—SENATOR KAMALA D. HARRIS, FEBRUARY 16, 2017

citizenship for long-term undocumented residents who pay a penalty. Bush's position was consistent with federal law, which considers it a misdemeanor to enter the United States without proper documentation. A misdemeanor is a relatively minor crime punishable by a fine and/or a short jail term. This is distinct from a felony, which is a more serious crime punishable by a harsher sentence.

PRESIDENTIAL POWER

Other people oppose DACA for entirely different reasons. They believe that immigration rules should come from Congress, rather than from presidential orders. Obama introduced DACA through an executive order rather than through a law passed by Congress. Obama made the choice to postpone legal action, such as deportation, against Dreamers. Some people argue that Obama's

Mitch McConnell is married to Elaine Chao, who is an immigrant from Taiwan. Chao is the US secretary of transportation.

actions weren't legal, and that DACA needed approval from Congress. A Republican senator from Kentucky, Mitch McConnell, disagreed with Obama's decision to implement DACA: "President Obama wrongly believed he had the authority to re-write our immigration law."[7] People who disagree with DACA for this reason note that a complete immigration reform, done by Congress, would be best for US immigration policy.

LANGUAGE IN THE MEDIA

The language used by politicians and journalists when they discuss the topic of undocumented immigrants can influence the way their readers or listeners think about it.

Patrick Buchanan was an adviser to three US presidents and is the author of *State of Emergency: The Third World Invasion and Conquest of America*. In his book he writes, "most of those [immigrants] coming are breaking in. They have no right to be here. . . . We are talking about an invasion."[8] The words *breaking in* imply a crime. Similarly, the word *invasion* is often associated with a military attack where people need to fight off the invaders. The point of such language is to stir up anger against immigrants and attempt to keep them out.

Many DACA supporters, including Obama, believe that when a family is in the United States without documentation, the children in that family are not responsible for the situation. As Obama put it

MEDIA AND IMMIGRATION

Media outlets differ widely in how they cover questions about immigration. This is often heard in language they use to describe undocumented immigrants. Fox News and the website Breitbart are conservative outlets. They tend to favor restrictions on immigration, deportations, and cancellation of the DACA policy. Fox News uses the term *illegal immigrant* often, which many people view as a way to dehumanize immigrants.

Other media outlets, such as the Associated Press and the Wall Street Journal, use biased language that clearly shows support for DACA. Journalist Krista Kafer of the *Denver Post* said, "I wonder how anyone can independently arrive at an opinion regarding DACA given the pro-DACA media coverage. It isn't that journalists are reporting incorrect facts. It's how they are arranging the facts to create a subtle narrative complete with protagonists and antagonists."[9]

in September 2017, "Whatever concerns or complaints Americans may have about immigration in general, we shouldn't threaten the future of this group of young people who are here through no fault of their own, who pose no threat, who are not taking away anything from the rest of us."[10]

Some critics of both DACA and other immigration reforms measure any immigration reform by whether it stops or lessens undocumented immigration. They want a policy that leads to fewer immigrants. The Trump administration agrees, and it has tried to end DACA.

US border patrol agents search for immigrants who crossed the US–Mexico border illegally.

FROM THE HEADLINES

IMMIGRATION AND CRIME

The Trump administration has claimed that immigrants bring an increase of crime, and supporters of deportations often echo these claims. However, several studies have shown that there is no increase. According to a CATO Institute study looking at arrest and conviction statistics from Texas in 2015, fewer immigrants than US-born residents were convicted of violent crimes. In fact, a study carried out throughout the United States between 1990 and 2014 found that undocumented immigration not only does not correlate to any increase in violent crime, it actually correlates to a slight decrease. In addition, a 2017 study published in the *Journal of Research and Practice* researched the same period. The authors of the study found evidence that an increase in undocumented immigration may have correlated to a decrease in drug use and driving under the influence. Another study explored the connections between immigration and crime in cities between 1970 and 2010. This study, published in the *Journal of Ethnicity in Criminal Justice* in 2017, did not distinguish between documented

Native-born Americans are more likely to be imprisoned than undocumented immigrants.

and undocumented immigration. However, like the other studies, it found that increases in immigration consistently coincided with decreases in both violent crime and property crime.

CHAPTER SEVEN

DACA'S EFFECT AND CANCELLATION

DACA has had a dramatic effect on the lives of many people. DACA recipients have been able to find jobs, obtain drivers' licenses, go to college, and receive better health care. Studies also show that recipients experience less stress than they did prior to receiving DACA status. Less stress typically translates directly into better health.

In 2017, Wong carried out a survey of more than 3,000 DACA recipients. He found that approximately 55.9 percent of people surveyed said that they were unemployed prior to DACA, whereas 91.4 percent

President Donald Trump has taken a hard stance against illegal immigration.

reported being employed after receiving DACA status. In addition, 68.5 percent of them reported finding a job with better pay and benefits, and 54.2 percent found jobs that were related to their education and training. About 70.8 percent of DACA recipients reported earning more money and being able to help their families financially.

Also, 5.4 percent of them reported starting a business and 15.7 percent reported buying a home.[1]

More than one-half of DACA recipients in Wong's study reported that DACA allowed them to pursue educational opportunities that were previously impossible for them. Approximately 52.5 percent of recipients in school at the time of the survey were pursuing a bachelor's degree, 19.4 percent were studying for an associate's degree, and 13.1 percent were

RECEIVING DACA STATUS

Rodrigo Trejo came to the United States from Mexico at age six. When he was in eleventh grade, his stepfather was deported. As his stepfather was leaving, he told Rodrigo that he believed he would not be able to come back. He died while crossing the border. Rodrigo became depressed after losing his stepdad, who had been his father figure. He also felt discouraged because he thought that being undocumented would mean he would never be able to go to college. These feelings led him to drop out of high school. He tried to get a job but was unable to because he was undocumented. Finally, he went back and finished high school. In 2014, he graduated from high school and received DACA status. Rodrigo planned to go to college and earn a degree in business.

in master's degree programs. An additional 3.6 percent were in doctoral programs and 2.3 percent were pursuing degrees in professions requiring special graduate training, such as medicine or law.[2] The rest of the recipients were pursuing a high school level education or a vocational program, or chose not to respond to the question.

Wong's was not the only survey on how DACA changed people's lives—at least three other surveys had similar results. Roberto G. Gonzales is a professor at Harvard University. Before DACA, he interviewed young, undocumented immigrants. He heard their pain over having no way to get a driver's license or funding for college. They talked about chronic headaches, sleeping trouble, ulcers, eating disorders, and severe depression. Then, after the program began,

"I WAS DETERMINED TO PROVE THAT MY CONTRIBUTIONS TO THIS COUNTRY WERE WORTHWHILE AND TO CHALLENGE THE NARRATIVE THAT THE UNDOCUMENTED COMMUNITY IS A BURDEN TO SOCIETY. WE WERE HERE TO STRENGTHEN THE FABRIC OF THIS GREAT NATION. . . . PERSONALLY, DACA HAS GIVEN ME A GLIMPSE OF LIFE AS A LAWFULLY PRESENT AMERICAN. THE THRILL OF PASSING MY LEARNER'S PERMIT TEST, OF BEING ASKED TO COME IN FOR A JOB INTERVIEW, OR EVEN OF THE SATISFACTION I FELT WHEN I SUBMITTED MY TAXES ON TIME— THESE SMALL INSTANCES FELT TREMENDOUSLY REWARDING."[3]

—GABRIELA GOMEZ, A DACA RECIPIENT

Gonzales found that DACA had a role in improving the mental health of Dreamers.

OVERTURNING DACA

President Trump entered office in January 2017 on a promise to end DACA, build a wall between the United States and Mexico, and decrease overall immigration.

During his first week in office, he issued an order to detain and deport undocumented immigrants in higher numbers than ever before. In addition, he introduced a travel ban to stop immigration from certain majority-Muslim countries.

On September 5, 2017, the Trump administration announced the end of DACA. Trump said, "I do not favor punishing children, most of whom are now adults, for the actions of their parents. But we

TRUMP'S TRAVEL BAN

After Trump became president in 2017, his administration tried various ways to restrict immigration from Muslim countries. Trump issued a travel ban on people coming to the United States from specific—predominantly Muslim—countries. The original ban included people from Iran, Iraq, Libya, Somalia, Sudan, Syria, and Yemen.

Trump's ban faced court challenges. One federal court in Virginia ruled that the ban was "unconstitutionally tainted with animus toward Islam."[4] However, in June 2018 the US Supreme Court upheld a new version of Trump's travel ban. The countries included on the revised travel ban were Iran, Libya, North Korea, Somalia, Syria, Venezuela, and Yemen.

DACA supporters protested outside the US Capitol building after the Trump
administration announced the end of the DACA program.

must also recognize that we are a nation of opportunity

because we are a nation of laws."[5]

DACA applications filed by September 5 would still be

considered and the government would accept renewals

until October 5, 2017. However, the government grants

DACA status for two years at a time, and when recipients

lose their status, they will become eligible for deportation.

In other words, they will not all be deported immediately,

but gradually, in the course of two years, everyone will

lose protection. Once they lose protection, ICE will be able

to deport them. The risk of deportation is of particular

concern because of the Trump policy directing ICE to

ZERO TOLERANCE IMMIGRATION

Trump took a zero tolerance policy on immigration after becoming president. He ordered the US government to charge immigrants with a crime for illegally entering the country. Between early 2018 and June 2018, this led to the separation of thousands of children and parents at the US–Mexico border, because children couldn't go to jail with their parents. This policy led to a public outroar of disapproval. In June, Trump ordered this practice to stop. Months later, many but not all of the separated families had been reunited.

deport any immigrant lacking proper documentation. Under the Obama administration, ICE focused on deporting undocumented immigrants who were convicted of serious criminal felonies or of multiple demeanors. Immigrant groups and civil rights groups immediately went to court to challenge Trump's decision to end DACA.

After the announcement to end DACA, the *Los Angeles Times* reported that up to eight million people could become targets for deportation.[6] The paper warned that this could mean breaking up families, undermining businesses that market primarily to immigrants, and leaving crops to rot—because many large agricultural companies rely on undocumented immigrants to harvest their crops.

On January 9, 2018, Federal Judge William Alsup ordered the US Department of Homeland Security to

MORE TO THE
STORY

PARENTS PUSHED OUT

Paola Benefo is a DACA recipient from Ghana, a country in West Africa. She came to the United States when she was four years old. In 2012, her father was deported. She writes, "His absence was unbearable, and the confusion and shame that came with it eroded my confidence. . . . Most of my friends . . . had no way of understanding what I was going through, and I worried many would actually approve of the government's tearing our family apart."[7]

In December 2015, Benefo's mother's lawyer called to say that her mother was facing deportation hearings and needed an affidavit supporting her request to stay. An affidavit is an official document with information that the writer swears to or affirms in writing in front of a notary public, who signs and seals the document. "Should I write about how my father was the one who pushed me in my studies, while my mother brought life to everything else in my world? That she infused the lives of my sisters and me with Ghanaian culture and taught us how to cook traditional dishes?" The president of Berea College, where Benefo was studying, wrote an affidavit as well, but the judge decided to deport Benefo's mother anyway. "My sisters and I have no family home," Benefo writes.[8]

begin accepting applications for DACA renewals while people waited for the courts to hear a legal challenge to the order ending the program. Alsup reasoned that hundreds of thousands of people had gone to considerable trouble to get DACA status and were living their lives on the basis of that status. He noted that losing that status would cause irreparable harm, because DACA recipients would no longer be able to live and work in the United States legally. The US Department of Homeland Security began processing the renewal applications, although the Trump administration announced that it would challenge the judgment. On January 16, 2018, the administration announced that it was asking the Supreme Court to intervene, but the Supreme Court turned down the request.

Also in January 2018, the Senate needed to vote on a bill to renew funding for the government. Senate Democrats insisted on including protections for Dreamers in that bill. Trump had a meeting on January 11 with senators and representatives from both parties to discuss immigration and try to reach agreement. At the meeting, Trump objected to the idea of protections for immigrants

Democratic lawmakers held a press conference in September 2017. They encouraged Republican lawmakers to argue against Trump's decision to end DACA.

from Haiti, El Salvador, and certain African countries. He asked, "Why do we want people from Haiti here?" and suggested that immigrants should come from Norway instead.[9] A United Nations spokesperson responded, "There is no other word one can use but racist. You cannot dismiss entire countries and continents . . . whose entire populations, who are not white are therefore not welcome."[10]

No agreement on protecting the Dreamers followed that meeting. In addition, the Republican leadership in the Senate brought the spending bill to the floor with no protections for the Dreamers. In response, some Republican senators and all of the Democrats in the Senate voted against the spending bill. On January 20, 2018, the government officially shut down due to lack of funding because the bill had not passed. Two days later, after Senator McConnell agreed to allow debate on a bill to protect the Dreamers, the Senate voted in favor of the spending bill, and government offices reopened.

On January 24, 2018, Trump proposed a path to citizenship for up to 1.8 million Dreamers.[11] In exchange, he wanted funding for his border wall, harsher crackdowns on other undocumented immigrants, and an end to visas for

During a government shutdown, nonessential departments are closed. This includes national monuments such as the Statue of Liberty.

the close relatives of people already living in the country and documented either as citizens or with visas. Although Trump claimed that his offer was generous, immigration advocates, Democrats, and some Republicans dismissed it as an effort to close the country's borders altogether. Instead, legislators from both parties began negotiating with each other to try to come up with a new proposal.

On April 24, 2018, a federal judge ruled that the DACA protections had to continue and ordered the government to begin accepting new applications again in addition to renewals. However, in August 2018 another judge said the government did not have to accept new DACA applications but had to process renewals. Various lawsuits both supporting and trying to end DACA continued to work through the courts.

FROM THE
HEADLINES

DEPORTATIONS

In 2017, the Trump administration ordered ICE to begin arresting immigrants without documentation even if they had committed no criminal violations. This was a dramatic change from previous policy. Altogether, ICE arrested 30 percent more people in 2017 than it did in 2016.[12] In 2018, more ICE arrests continued.

ICE officers often imprison the people they have stopped until the deportation can proceed. If the immigrants are applying for asylum, an asylum officer interviews them to assess whether they face a real risk of harm because of their political beliefs, religion, race, or social group in their home country.

Immigrants face a hearing in front of a judge. If they are approved for deportation, people are taken to a location with others facing deportation to the same country. They are handcuffed. Their ankles are also cuffed and their hands are chained to their waists. They each have one see-through plastic bag with their belongings. Armed guards go with them on the flight back to their countries of origin. Some people are deported to countries that they no longer remember, whose language they may not speak if they came to the United States as small children.

2017 DEPORTATIONS[13]

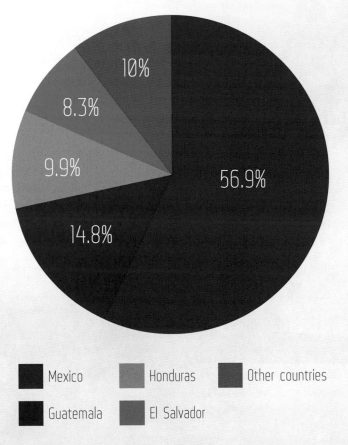

10%

8.3%

9.9%

56.9%

14.8%

■ Mexico   ■ Honduras   ■ Other countries

■ Guatemala   ■ El Salvador

*Numbers do not equal 100% because of rounding.

The majority of people deported in 2017 went to Mexico and countries in Central America.

CHAPTER EIGHT

THE FUTURE
OF DACA

After the Trump administration announced its decision on DACA, Obama responded:

Immigration can be a controversial topic. We all want safe, secure borders and a dynamic economy, and people of goodwill can have legitimate disagreements about how to fix our immigration system. . . . But that's not what the action that the White House took today is about. This is about young people who grew up in America—kids who study in our schools, young adults who are starting careers, patriots who pledge allegiance to our flag. . . . To target these young people is wrong—because they have done nothing wrong.[1]

In addition, some Republican lawmakers disagreed with Trump's decision. Senator John McCain said, "President Trump's decision to eliminate DACA is the wrong approach to immigration policy. . . . I strongly

Dreamers and their supporters marched in Washington, DC, in March 2018. They asked lawmakers to come up with a legislative fix for DACA.

"ARE WE A NATION THAT TOLERATES THE HYPOCRISY OF A SYSTEM WHERE WORKERS WHO PICK OUR FRUIT AND MAKE OUR BEDS NEVER HAVE A CHANCE TO GET RIGHT WITH THE LAW? OR ARE WE A NATION THAT GIVES THEM A CHANCE TO MAKE AMENDS, TAKE RESPONSIBILITY, AND GIVE THEIR KIDS A BETTER FUTURE?"[4]

—PRESIDENT BARACK OBAMA, 2014

believe that children who were illegally brought into this country through no fault of their own should not be forced to return to a country they do not know."[2] Even people who disagreed with Obama's executive order in 2012 wanted to protect the Dreamers. US representative Cathy McMorris Rodgers, a Republican, said, "I've long said I didn't agree with the way the previous administration went about enacting DACA, but we must protect children who are already here in this country and those who are currently protected under DACA. . . . We must work in Congress to provide a long-term certainty for DACA recipients."[3]

Others agreed that a change needed to be made regarding immigration. Republican US representative Paul Ryan said, "At the heart of this issue are young people who came to this country through no fault of their own. . . . Their status is one of many immigration issues, such as border security and interior enforcement. . . . It is

MORE TO THE
STORY

AN IMMIGRANT'S ADVOCACY

Martín Batalla Vidal moved to New York City from Mexico just as he was beginning school. He was one of four brothers raised by a single mother. He didn't find out that he was undocumented until he was preparing to graduate high school and starting to think about college. Without financial aid, he knew going to college would be impossible. But after high school graduation, he began working to save money for college.

Vidal was afraid to apply for DACA at first, but he finally applied in 2015. At the time, the Obama administration had just extended the work permits granted under DACA from two to three years, but 26 states sued the federal government to block this change.[5] In response, the federal government revoked it. Vidal joined up with three immigrant advocacy organizations to try to get the three-year work permits restored. At the same time, he started taking college classes and earning more at his job. As of 2017, Vidal was taking college classes, working in a nursing home, and working with advocacy organizations to challenge the Trump administration's plans to end DACA.

my hope that the House and Senate, with the president's leadership, will be able to find consensus on a permanent legislative solution."[6]

As of September 2018, it was not clear how the situation surrounding DACA would resolve. Since the 2018 federal judge's ruling that the US Department of Homeland Security should begin renewing DACA applications again, it looked possible that DACA could survive through 2018 in some capacity because of judicial action.

A general sense exists that a new comprehensive law that protects the Dreamers, provides a path to citizenship for a broad group of undocumented immigrants, and addresses other immigration issues would be helpful. After

DACA activists shut down Independence Avenue in Washington, DC, as part of their March 2018 protests.

Trump's decision to end DACA, lawmakers began looking at ways to compromise with each other on immigration legislation. In June 2018, House Republicans came out with a draft of an immigration bill that would give Dreamers protections while also giving $23.4 billion for a US–Mexico border wall.[7] However, the bill failed after a 121–301 vote.[8]

THE TRUMP WHITE HOUSE

The Trump White House website on immigration no longer mentions DACA or the Dreamers. Instead, it talks about building "a border wall and ensuring the swift removal of unlawful entrants."[9] It also discusses restricting legal immigration by ending family-based immigration and the Green Card Lottery.

RESEARCHING IMMIGRANT HISTORY

In the summer of 2017, journalist and genealogist Jennifer Mendelsohn started researching the family trees of people who were advocating against immigration. White House adviser Stephen Miller was one of the people behind Trump's tough immigration policy. He has advocated preferential treatment for English-speaking immigrants. Mendelsohn discovered a 1910 US Census record and found that Miller's great-grandmother didn't speak English. And when the White House social media director, Dan Scavino, tweeted against chain migration, Mendelsohn found that his ancestors came from Italy through chain migration. Mendelsohn notes that she does this research to remind people of their immigrant history: "It shows how universal immigration is in so many American stories. Some people who've been in the country longer, it may not feel that close and it's easy for them to forget."[10]

Family-based immigration is when a close relative of a permanent resident or citizen may move to the United States. The Green Card Lottery allows people from any country from which fewer than 50,000 immigrants have entered the United States in the past five years to apply for a green card. The random lottery process selects 50,000 applicants each year.[11] Congress created this program in 1990 in order to increase immigrant diversity, and it is also called the Diversity Immigrant Visa Program.

US IMMIGRATION AND DACA

Immigration reform is a topic that's often debated in the United States. The many viewpoints include protecting undocumented immigrants already in the United States, enhancing border security in an attempt to protect citizens, and being more selective about which immigrants should be able to come to the United States. In 2016, there were approximately 11.3 million undocumented immigrants in the United States.[12] In 2018, approximately 1.3 million people would have been eligible to apply for DACA.[13]

Lawmakers—such as Senator Cory Booker, *right*—have met with Dreamers to show their support.

Some young Dreamers are doing their part to fight against prejudices and stereotypes surrounding undocumented immigrants. Many Dreamers speak publicly about the opportunities given to them through DACA. They reflect on the lives they've built and look toward a future that may not have been possible for them without the DACA program. Riya Nathrani is one DACA recipient who spoke out about how DACA changed her life: "DACA has provided me with countless opportunities to financially support myself, my education, and my family. . . . DACA changed my life for the better."[14]

ESSENTIAL
FACTS

MAJOR EVENTS

- Republican Senator Orrin Hatch of Utah first introduced the bipartisan Development, Relief and Education for Alien Minors (DREAM) Act in 2001. It never passed, although the act has been reintroduced many times in many different versions. All versions would allow certain undocumented immigrants who arrived in the United States as children younger than a certain age to legalize their status.

- On June 15, 2012, President Barack Obama announced the DACA program. If the Dreamers' applications were approved, they couldn't be deported for two years. An approved application would also allow Dreamers to apply for work visas.

- In 2017, the Trump administration announced its decision to end DACA. Various legal challenges were immediately brought up to fight this decision.

KEY PLAYERS

- Barack Obama introduced the DACA program.

- Dreamers are people who were brought to the United States when they were children and have been long-term US residents. Many Dreamers came to the United States legally but either outstayed their visas or were unable to update them. DACA offers opportunities to Dreamers.

- Donald Trump worked to end the DACA program.

IMPACT ON SOCIETY

DACA has given many Dreamers the opportunity to realize their potential while in the United States. The DACA program also benefits the US economy, as many Dreamers pay taxes and start new businesses.

QUOTE

"Whatever concerns or complaints Americans may have about immigration in general, we shouldn't threaten the future of this group of young people who are here through no fault of their own, who pose no threat, who are not taking away anything from the rest of us."

—Barack Obama, 2017

GLOSSARY

ASSIMILATE
To adopt the ways of another culture.

ASYLUM
Protection given by a country to someone who has left his or her country as a political refugee.

BILINGUAL
Able to speak two languages fluently.

BIPARTISAN
Involving cooperation between the two major political parties.

HATE GROUP
A group that promotes prejudice against people with a specific identity or set of identities.

HUMANITARIAN
To be concerned with relieving human suffering.

INDENTURED SERVANT
A person contracted to work for a certain period of time, usually without pay.

INTERROGATE
To question closely, formally, and sometimes harshly.

LIBERTARIAN
Believing in the doctrine of free will and upholding liberty in thought and action.

NATURALIZATION
The process of obtaining citizenship.

STUDENT VISA
A document that allows a person to enter a country for purposes of study and to live in the country during the period of study.

VISA
An official authorization permitting entry into and travel within a country.

VOCATIONAL
Related to a trade, skill, or job.

ADDITIONAL
RESOURCES

SELECTED BIBLIOGRAPHY

Alden, Edward. *The Closing of the American Border*. Harper Collins, 2008.

Bennett, Brian. "Not Just 'Bad Hombres': Trump Is Targeting up to 8 Million People for Deportation." *Los Angeles Times*, 4 Feb. 2017, latimes.com. Accessed 20 Aug. 2018.

Noorani, Ali. *There Goes the Neighborhood*. Prometheus, 2017.

FURTHER READINGS

Carser, A. R. *US Immigration Policy*. Abdo, 2018.

Truax, Eileen. *Dreamers*. Beacon, 2015.

ONLINE RESOURCES

To learn more about the Dreamers and DACA, visit **abdobooklinks.com**. These links are routinely monitored and updated to provide the most current information available.

MORE INFORMATION

For more information on this subject, contact or visit the following organizations:

United We Dream
unitedwedream.org
United We Dream is led by immigrant youth to provide resources for young immigrants to advocate for themselves.

US Citizenship and Immigration Services
111 Massachusetts Ave. NW, MS 2260
Washington, DC 20529-2260
800-375-5283
uscis.gov
This website provides information on citizenship applications as well as archived content relating to the DACA program.

SOURCE
NOTES

CHAPTER 1. A STORY OF A DREAMER

1. "Pratishtha Khanna." *American Federation of Teachers*, n.d., aft.org. Accessed 29 Aug. 2018.

2. "Pratishtha Khanna."

3. "Remarks by the President in Address to the Nation on Immigration." *White House*, 20 Nov. 2014, obamawhitehouse.archives.gov. Accessed 29 Aug. 2018.

4. "Deferred Action for Childhood Arrivals (DACA)." *White House Initiative on Asian Americans and Pacific Islanders*, n.d., sites.ed.gov. Accessed 29 Aug. 2018.

5. "Deferred Action for Childhood Arrivals (DACA)."

6. "Secretary Napolitano Announces Deferred Action Process for Young People Who Are Low Enforcement Priorities." *US Department of Homeland Security*, 15 June 2012, dhs.gov. Accessed 29 Aug. 2018.

7. Tom Jawetz, et al. "Dreams Deferred: A Lock at DACA Renewals and Losses Post–March 5." *Center for American Progress*, 2 Mar. 2018, americanprogress.org. Accessed 29 Aug. 2018.

8. "Deferred Action for Childhood Arrivals (DACA)."

CHAPTER 2. WHO ARE THE DREAMERS?

1. "DREAM Act." *Congress.gov*, n.d., congress.gov. Accessed 29 Aug. 2018.

2. "House Passes 'DREAM Act' Immigration Bill." *Reuters*, 8 Dec. 2018, reuters.com. Accessed 29 Aug. 2018.

3. "Remarks by the President on Immigration." *White House*, 15 June 2012, obamawhitehouse.archives.gov. Accessed 29 Aug. 2018.

4. Audrey Singer and Nicole Prchal Svajlenka. "Immigration Facts: Deferred Action for Childhood Arrivals (DACA)." *Metropolitan Policy Program at Brookings*, 14 Aug. 2013, brookings.edu. Accessed 29 Aug. 2018.

CHAPTER 3. UNDOCUMENTED

1. Arturo Garcia. "NPR Anchor Ties Term 'Illegal Immigrant' to Nazi Germany." *Raw Story*, 7 Oct. 2012, rawstory.com. Accessed 29 Aug. 2018.

2. Jo Tuckman. "'Flee or Die': Violence Drives Central America's Child Migrants to US Border." *Guardian*, 9 July 2014, theguardian.com. Accessed 29 Aug. 2018.

3. "Countries with the Highest and Lowest Crime Rates." *Clements*, n.d., clements.com. Accessed 29 Aug. 2018.

4. "Murder." *FBI: UCR*, n.d., ucr.fbi.gov. Accessed 29 Aug. 2018.

5. "A Guide to International Refugee Protection and Building State Asylum Systems." *UNHCR*, 2017, unhcr.org. Accessed 29 Aug. 2018.

6. "Entry/Exit Overstay Report." *US Department of Homeland Security*, 19 Jan. 2016, dhs.gov. Accessed 29 Aug. 2018.

7. "Fiscal Year 2016 Entry/Exit Overstay Report." *US Department of Homeland Security*, n.d., dhs.gov. Accessed 29 Aug. 2018.

8. Danika Fears and Lorena Mongelli. "Why Central Americans Are Fleeing Their Violent Homelands for the US." *New York Post*, 13 Apr. 2017, nypost.com. Accessed 29 Aug. 2018.

9. "Illegal? Better If You're Irish." *LA Times*, 8 Apr. 2007, latimes.com. Accessed 29 Aug. 2018.

10. "Jose Manuel Santoyo." *FWD*, n.d., fwd.us. Accessed 29 Aug. 2018.

11. Jens Manuel Krogstad et al. "5 Facts about Illegal Immigration in the U.S." *Pew Research Center*, 27 Apr. 2017, pewresearch.org. Accessed 29 Aug. 2018.

12. Krogstad et al. "5 Facts about Illegal Immigration in the U.S."

CHAPTER 4. A HISTORY OF IMMIGRATION

1. "A Century of Lawmaking for a New Nation: US Congressional Documents and Debates, 1774–1875." *Library of Congress*, n.d., loc.gov. Accessed 29 Aug. 2018.

2. Henry Louis Gates Jr. "How Many Slaves Landed in the U.S.?" *PBS*, n.d., pbs.org. Accessed 29 Aug. 2018.

3. "Africans in America." *Library of Congress*, n.d., loc.gov. Accessed 29 Aug. 2018.

4. "Irish-Catholic Immigration to America." *Library of Congress*, n.d., loc.gov. Accessed 29 Aug. 2018.

5. Mark Bulik. "1854: No Irish Need Apply." *New York Times*, 8 Sept. 2015, nytimes.com. Accessed 29 Aug. 2018.

6. John F. Kennedy. *A Nation of Immigrants*. Harper & Row, 1986. 23.

7. Joel Mokyr. "Great Famine." *Encyclopedia Britannica*, n.d., britannica.com. Accessed 29 Aug. 2018.

8. Kennedy, *A Nation of Immigrants*, 58.

9. Erika Lee. *The Making of Asian America: A History*. Simon & Schuster, 2015. 59.

10. Margaret Sands Orchowski. *The Law That Changed the Face of America: The Immigration and Nationality Act of 1965*. Rowman & Littlefield, 2015. 32.

11. Orchowski, *The Law That Changed the Face of America*, 37.

12. Orchowski, *The Law That Changed the Face of America*, 46.

13. Kennedy, *A Nation of Immigrants*, 78.

14. Kennedy, *A Nation of Immigrants*, 79.

15. Henry Bischoff. *Immigration Issues*. Greenwood, 2002. 92.

16. "Immigration and Nationality Act of 1965." *Immigration to the United States*, n.d., immigrationtounitedstates.org. Accessed 29 Aug. 2018.

17. Kennedy, *A Nation of Immigrants*, 63.

18. Don Gonyea. "The GOP's Evolution on Immigration." *NPR*, 25 Jan. 2018, npr.org. Accessed 29 Aug. 2018.

19. Tom Templeton and Tom Lumley. "9/11 in Numbers." *Guardian*, 17 Aug. 2002, theguardian.com. Accessed 29 Aug. 2018.

CHAPTER 5. VIEWS ON IMMIGRATION

1. John Burnett. "Explaining 'Chain Migration.'" *NPR*, 7 Jan. 2018, npr.org. Accessed 30 Aug. 2018.

2. John F. Kennedy. *A Nation of Immigrants*. Harper & Row, 1986. 69.

3. Benjamin Harris. "Why Your Economic Argument against Immigration Is Probably Wrong." *Fortune*, 11 Sept. 2017, fortune.com. Accessed 30 Aug. 2018.

4. Ann H. Coulter. *Adios, America*. Regnery, 2015.

5. Gustavo López and Kristen Bialik. "Key Findings about U.S. Immigrants." *Pew Research Center*, 3 May 2017, pewresearch.org. Accessed 30 Aug. 2018.

6. Jeremy Diamond. "Donald Trump: Ban All Muslim Travel to U.S." *CNN*, 8 Dec. 2015, cnn.com. Accessed 30 Aug. 2018.

7. Ali Noorani. *There Goes the Neighborhood: How Communities Overcome Prejudice and Meet the Challenge of American Immigration*. Prometheus, 2017. 40.

SOURCE NOTES
CONTINUED

8. Alex Nowrasteh and Robert Orr. "Immigration and the Welfare State: Immigrant and Native Use Rates and Benefit Levels for Means-Tested Welfare and Entitlement Programs." *CATO Institute*, 10 May 2018, cato.org. Accessed 30 Aug. 2018.

9. "Immigrants and the Economy." *ACLU*, n.d., aclu.org. Accessed 30 Aug. 2018.

10. Stuart Anderson. "Immigrants and Billion Dollar Startups." *National Foundation for American Policy*, March 2016, nfap.com. Accessed 30 Aug. 2018.

11. "Deferred Action for Childhood Arrivals (DACA)." *White House Initiative on Asian Americans and Pacific Islanders*, n.d., sites.ed.gov. Accessed 30 Aug. 2018.

CHAPTER 6. ARGUMENTS FOR AND AGAINST DACA

1. Jennifer De Pinto. "Most Americans Support DACA, but Oppose Border Wall—CBS News Poll." *CBS News*, 18 Jan. 2018, cbsnews.com. Accessed 30 Aug. 2018.

2. Ilya Somin. "The Case for Keeping DACA." *Washington Post*, 4 Sept. 2017, washingtonpost.com. Accessed 30 Aug. 2018.

3. Elizabeth Chmurak. "The Economic Impact of Losing DACA Workers." *NBC News*, 6 Mar. 2018, nbcnews.com. Accessed 30 Aug. 2018.

4. Kathryn Watson. "Koch Brothers Try to Navigate Differences with Trump Going into 2018 Elections." *CBS News*, 7 Feb. 2018, cbsnews.com. Accessed 30 Aug. 2018.

5. Kris Kobach. "The Senate Immigration Bill Rewards Lawbreaking: Why the DREAM Act Is a Nightmare." *Heritage Foundation*, 14 Aug. 2006, heritage.org. Accessed 30 Aug. 2018.

6. Michelle Ye Hee Lee. "Sen. Kamala Harris's Claim That an 'Undocumented Immigrant Is Not a Criminal.'" *Washington Post*, 26 Apr. 2017, washingtonpost.com. Accessed 30 Aug. 2018.

7. Daniella Diaz and Lauren Fox. "Democrats Slam the End of DACA, while Republicans Are Mixed." *CNN*, 5 Sept. 2017, cnn.com. Accessed 30 Aug. 2018.

8. Patrick J. Buchanan. *State of Emergency: The Third World Invasion and Conquest of America*. St. Martin's, 2006. 221.

9. Krista Kafer. "In Coverage of DACA, Journalists' Biases Are Showing." *Denver Post*, 7 Sept. 2017, denverpost.com. Accessed 30 Aug. 2018.

10. Kevin Liptak. "Obama Slams Trump for Rescinding DACA, Calls Move 'Cruel.'" *CNN*, 5 Sept. 2017, cnn.com. Accessed 30 Aug. 2018.

CHAPTER 7. DACA'S EFFECT AND CANCELLATION

1. Tom K. Wong et al. "Results from Tom K. Wong et al., 2017 National DACA Study." *Center for American Progress*, n.d., cdn.americanprogress.org. Accessed 30 Aug. 2018.

2. Wong, "Results from Tom K. Wong et al., 2017 National DACA Study."

3. Gabriela Gomez. "How DACA Changed My Life." *Huffington Post*, 11 Sept. 2014, huffingtonpost.com. Accessed 30 Aug. 2018.

4. Subha Varadarajan. "Trump's Latest Muslim Ban Makes Its Way to the Supreme Court." *National Immigration Law Center*, 2 Apr. 2018, nilc.org. Accessed 30 Aug. 2018.

5. Adam Kelsey and Veronica Stracqualursi. "Lawmakers, Organizations Speak Out after Trump's Decision to End DACA." *ABC News*, 5 Sept. 2017, abcnews.go.com. Accessed 30 Aug. 2018.

6. Brian Bennett. "Not Just 'Bad Hombres': Trump Is Targeting up to 8 Million People for Deportation." *Los Angeles Times*, 4 Feb. 2017, latimes.com. Accessed 30 Aug. 2018.

7. Paola Benefo. "What It's Like to Have Your Parents Deported." *New York Times*, 27 Feb. 2017, nytimes.com. Accessed 30 Aug. 2018.

8. Benefo, "What It's Like to Have Your Parents Deported."

9. Julie Hirschfeld et al. "Trump Alarms Lawmakers with Disparaging Words for Haiti and Africa." *New York Times*, 11 Jan. 2018, nytimes.com. Accessed 30 Aug. 2018.

10. Patrick Wintour et al. "'There's No Other Word but Racist.'" *Guardian*, 13 Jan. 2018, theguardian.com. Accessed 30 Aug. 2018.

11. Michael D. Shear and Sheryl Gay Stolberg. "Trump Immigration Plan Demands Tough Concessions from Democrats." *New York Times*, 25 Jan. 2018, nytimes.com. Accessed 30 Aug. 2018.

12. Christina Caron. "Michigan Father Deported after Living in U.S. for 30 Years." *New York Times*, 16 Jan. 2018, nytimes.com. Accessed 30 Aug. 2018.

13. John Burnett. "Undocumented Irish Caught in Trump's Immigration Dragnet." *NPR*, 22 Jan. 2018, npr.org. Accessed 30 Aug. 2018.

CHAPTER 8. THE FUTURE OF DACA

1. Barack Obama. "Immigration Can Be a Controversial Topic." *Facebook*, 5 Sept. 2017, facebook.com. Accessed 30 Aug. 2018.

2. Daniella Diaz and Lauren Fox. "Democrats Slam the End of DACA, While Republicans Are Mixed." *CNN*, 5 Sept. 2017, cnn.com. Accessed 30 Aug. 2018.

3. Diaz and Fox, "Democrats Slam the End of DACA, While Republicans Are Mixed."

4. "Transcript: President Obama's Immigration Address." *CNN*, 21 Nov. 2014, cnn.com. Accessed 30 Aug. 2018.

5. Martín Batalla Vidal. "DACA Changed My Life. I'm Suing the Trump Administration to Save It." *Washington Post*, 6 Sept. 2017, washingtonpost.com. Accessed 30 Aug. 2018.

6. Kathryn Watson. "Congress Reacts to Trump Ending DACA." *CBS News*, 5 Sept. 2017, cbsnews.com. Accessed 30 Aug. 2018.

7. Eliza Collins and Deirdre Shesgreen. "House GOP Releases Compromise Immigration Legislation That Would Protect 'Dreamers,' Fund Wall." *USA Today*, 14 June 2018, usatoday.com. Accessed 30 Aug. 2018.

8. Lauren Fox. "Republican-Leadership Backed Immigration Bill Goes Down in Flames." *CNN*, 27 June 2018, cnn.com. Accessed 30 Aug. 2018.

9. "Immigration." *White House*, n.d., whitehouse.gov. Accessed 30 Aug. 2018.

10. AJ Willingham. "They Spoke Out against Immigrants. So She Unearthed Their Own Immigrant Ancestors." *CNN*, 23 June 2018, cnn.com. Accessed 30 Aug. 2018.

11. "The Diversity Immigrant Visa Program: An Overview." *American Immigration Council*, 13 Nov. 2017, americanimmigrationcouncil.org. Accessed 30 Aug. 2018.

12. Alan Gomez. "Undocumented Immigrant Population in U.S. Stays Flat for Eighth Straight Year." *USA Today*, 25 Apr. 2017, usatoday.com. Accessed 30 Aug. 2018.

13. Lori Robertson. "The Facts on DACA." *FactCheck.org*, 22 Jan. 2018, factcheck.org. Accessed 30 Aug. 2018.

14. "We 'Finally Feel at Home': How DACA Has Changed Lives across America." *NBC News*, 15 June 2016, nbcnews.com. Accessed 30 Aug. 2018.

INDEX

ABOUT THE
AUTHORS

DUCHESS HARRIS, JD, PHD

Professor Harris is the chair of the American Studies department at Macalester College and curator of the Duchess Harris Collection of ABDO books. She is the author and coauthor of recently released ABDO books including *Hidden Human Computers: The Black Women of NASA*, *Black Lives Matter*, and *Race and Policing*.

Before working with ABDO, she authored several other books on the topics of race, culture, and American history. She served as an associate editor for *Litigation News*, the American Bar Association Section of Litigation's quarterly flagship publication, and was the first editor in chief of *Law Raza*, an interactive online journal covering race and the law, published at William Mitchell College of Law. She has earned a PhD in American Studies from the University of Minnesota and a JD from William Mitchell College of Law.

NINA JUDITH KATZ

Nina Judith Katz is a writer, editor, lexicographer, and word nerd. She served as associate editor of the *American Heritage Dictionary, Third Edition*. Nina is also an herbalist, forager, and shiatsu therapist.